How to Build Custom-made Handcrafted Fishing Rods

And Repair or Customize Your Favorite Rod

By John B. Emery

Edited by Mark J. Sosin
Photography by Robert D. Stearns
Rods Built by Capt. Al Forest

 Publishing, Inc.

105 NE 25th St.   P.O. Box 371005   Miami, Fl. 33137

ISBN 0-89317-024-0
Library of Congress No. 77-81170
1 3 5 7 9 10 8 6 4 2
Printed in the United States of America

Contents

Cover photo of jumping marlin courtesy of E. "Jo-Jo" Del Guercio, Jr. Photo by Bill Staros.

1. Getting Started

INTRODUCTION

Rod building is easy, fun, relaxing, and offers the challenge of a useful and unique hobby. When you build your own rods, you not only gain satisfaction from producing an attractive product, but you have the opportunity to create tackle specifically for your needs. There is no greater enjoyment in fishing than to cast accurately with a rod you designed, or to fight a fish on a stick that you put together. The money you save building your own rods enables you to use the best components and still pay much less than you would in the store, assuming, of course, that you could find a comparable rod.

Getting into rod building is simple. Components are available from many tackle shops and national distributors who specialize in rod building items ranging from blanks to guides, grips, and threads. These experts are willing to share their knowledge with you in selecting the right components and answer any questions you might have on construction techniques. We recommend that you place your confidence in a reputable firm and let them help you keep pace with the latest developments.

This manual has been designed to help you get started in rod building and to serve as a reference if you want to review any specific operation. Read the

Figure 1. Component specialists stock a full line of the latest items which are shipped all over the country.

5

pertinent sections carefully and completely *before* you start to build the rod. Then, go back and follow along step by step. Remember to take your time and work at your own pace. Allow ample time for glues and finishes to dry thoroughly. Many anglers prefer to begin by repairing and refinishing rods that have seen years of service. Other start with a completely new rod. Either way, you are about to embark on a satisfying and enjoyable experience.

THE WORK AREA

Rods can be built anywhere. All you need to get started is a clean work area and some basic tools that include a pair of U-shaped blocks of wood to support the rod blank so that you can turn it. These blocks can be clamped to the kitchen table, any other table, or to a workbench. You really don't need a great deal of space.

Figure 2. A pair of U-shaped blocks padded with cloth, felt, or foam support the rod. They can be clamped to a table or set up anywhere.

THREAD TENSION DEVICE

We prefer to regulate thread tension with our fingers, but many builders like to use a tension device to hold the thread so that both hands are free to turn the rod. Tension devices are sold commercially, but you can build your own easily by drilling a hole in a short length of wood, inserting a bolt, and using washers, a spring, and a wingnut to hold the spool of thread in place. Another simple method is to run the thread through a heavy book and add more books on top until the desired tension is achieved.

Figure 3. Insert a bolt through a board, add a couple of washers on either side of a spring, tighten with a wingnut, and you have a thread tension device.

BASIC TOOLS AND MATERIALS

You probably already have most of the basic tools you will need. If you don't, the investment is minimal. Here is the list.

Tools
1. Hacksaw blade or fine-toothed saw to cut blanks.
2. Three-cornered file for trimming blanks.
3. Round file or reamer to fit grips to the blank.
4. Marking pencil or felt-tip marker for indicating the spline or guide spacing on the blank.
5. Razor blades or fly-tying scissors for trimming thread.

Materials
1. Masking tape to mark blanks, hold guides in place prior to wrapping, and to make centering bushings for reel seats.
2. Good quality, two-part epoxy glue (preferably the thick, paste type) for securing grips, reel seats, butt caps, and wood or aluminum butts.
3. Hot melt-tip cement (often called ferrule cement) for gluing tiptops in place.

Figure 4. With a small motor and a foot pedal to control the speed, the rod builder can use both hands to work on the rod.

4. Nylon thread for wrapping the guides.
5. Finish for the windings.

The serious rod builder will eventually acquire additional equipment to save time and make the task easier. Some of the items would be:

1. Propane or butane torch for melting tip cement, removing old tips, and even removing broken reel seats that were glued into place.
2. A sewing machine motor with foot pedal speed control to turn the rod while wrapping or sanding and shaping grips.
3. Another motor for turning the rod when the finish is applied to insure that finish flows smoothly across the wrappings.
4. Standard workshop tools such as lathes, drills, saws, and other equipment that may prove handy from time to time, but are not necessary.

2. Selecting the Components

THE BLANK

Choosing the right blank with the proper action for the type of rod you intend to build is extremely important. The best advice we can offer is to suggest that you rely on expert advice from the component supplier until you develop a feel for the various blanks. If you tell your supplier what reel you intend to use, line test or flyline size, baits or lures you prefer, and the fish you are after, he can usually recommend blanks that have been tested and proven. Remember, that by trimming the butt or tip of a blank (or both), you can significantly alter the action.

Rod action is a term that basically describes where the blank bends. Slower action rods bend through a greater portion of the blank, while fast action limits bending to an area near the tip. In between, there is a wide range of actions available to the rod builder.

In considering the blank action, keep in mind that the key to whether a rod feels good in the hand may lie in where the weight is concentrated. Blanks with large diameter butts and light tips put most of the weight near the point where they are held while fishing. This makes them easy to handle and gives them a feeling of lightness in relation to stiffness. Slow-action rods sometimes feel heavy for their actual weight, because the mass is concentrated along the entire shaft, and there is more weight near the tip end. The feeling of heaviness often disappears when a reel is attached to the finished rod.

Tubular fiberglass is still the primary blank material, and designs have become extremely sophisticated. Modern blanks are extremely light weight and exceptionally strong. Solid glass blanks are available for building boat rods and bottom fishing rods. They are extremely durable, but they are also much heavier than tubular glass, and sacrifice action.

Graphite blanks have attracted the attention and captured the imagination of fishermen because they are smaller in diameter, lighter in weight, and quicker in response than fiberglass. The unique sensitivity of graphite, which permits better monitoring of bait or lure and superior casting, may be its most significant asset. Fly fishermen enjoy additional benefits from graphite, since it allows the design of longer rods for lines of the same weight.

As technology improves and new blank materials are introduced, the rod builder will continue to benefit from an impressive array of options. Qualified components dealers can keep you advised of the latest developments and recommend the most advanced blank for the type of rod you want to build.

GUIDES AND TIPTOPS

Ideally, a line guide should be light enough to complement the rod's action, strong enough to withstand heavy use, hard enough to resist wear, and smooth enough to avoid abrading the line. Guides should also be resistant to corrosion and deterioration by the elements.

Figure 5. Rod builders can choose from an impressive selection of blanks made of both fiberglass and graphite.

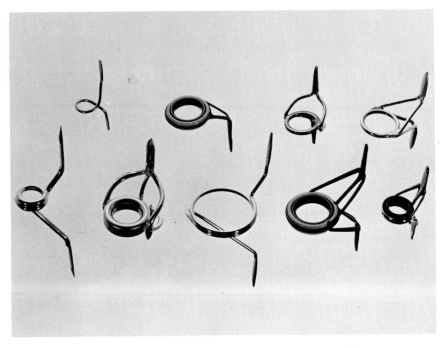

Figure 6. The weight of the guide and the degree of stiffness of its feet are important considerations in choosing the right combination for any rod. Component dealers usually stock a wide variety of styles and sizes.

The weight and the stiffness of each guide must be considered for the specific rod you are building. Heavy guides that don't flex, for example, can destroy the action of a light casting rod. On the other hand, husky rods often require heavier and stronger guides. Flexible foot guides usually follow the bending pattern of a rod better than fixed foot guides. In the case of spinning rods, the height of the guides above the blank is also important. If there isn't enough distance between the ring and the blank, the line could slap the blank on a cast, and you would lose distance.

The new shock-protected ceramic guides have become a favorite with rod builders. An almost diamond-hard, but brittle material is used for an inner ring and this is set in a softer, shock-absorbing outer ring for protection. Tests show that these guides are exceptionally smooth and they don't groove from normal use unless wire lines are used.

Hard chrome-plated, stainless steel guides are another good choice. Large size ceramic guides are heavy and impractical for big spinning and surf rods, making this a perfect application for hard chrome. There is a distinct difference between decorative chrome-plated guides and hard chrome-plated guides. Hard chrome has a very low coefficient of friction and will not groove easily, yet a lot of anglers avoid using it because they associate the hard chrome with regular decorative chrome plating which does groove.

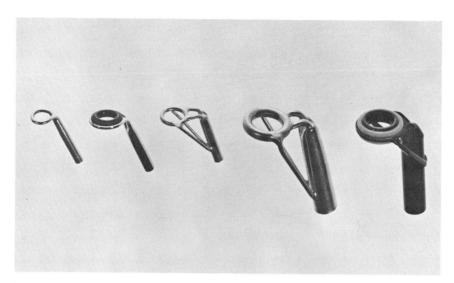

Figure 7. Tiptops are available to match any series of guides.

Tungsten carbide is probably more resistant to line grooving than any other material and has been popular with anglers for years. It is a difficult material to weld or solder, however, and is usually mounted in nickel silver which tends to corrode and turn green. A pinkish surface oxidation also forms on tungsten carbide causing line wear. This material is relatively brittle and delicate in slender rings, but extremely heavy in thicker rings. We consider tungsten carbide to be unsurpassed for use with wire line, but we do not recommend its use with other lines.

Roller guides will surpass any other type for preventing line wear. They are used exclusively on trolling rods where there is adequate stiffness to absorb the weight of the guides. If a rod will be used with lines lighter than 20-pound test (10 kilograms), check the clearances between rollers and the frames to make sure the line will not fall between them.

CORK GRIPS, STICKS, AND RINGS

Cork is the most popular material for fishing-rod grips, because it is light in weight, resilient, and comfortable to the hand. Rod builders have the option of using preshaped cork grips, sticks of cork made from rings, or the individual rings which are about ½ inch thick. The rings must be glued together on the blank and then shaped. Cork sticks must also be shaped.

Whether you choose grips, sticks, or rings, the density of the material determines the grade of cork, and the number of pores or voids is the primary factor in controlling the density. The more pores, the poorer the grade. Denser grades (especially in large diameters) take longer to grow and obviously will cost more. The best grades—superfine (almost non-existent these days) and extra select— can be shaped into grips without filling. Select and superior (the next two grades) often require some filling. Preshaped grips are made from standard-grade cork and are always filled. Custom grips are made from better grades of cork and are stocked by leading component suppliers.

Since the finest quality cork is only available in rings, many custom rod builders prefer to use the rings and shape their own grips.

CELLITE AND SYNTHETIC GRIPS

Synthetic rod grips made of Cellite, Hypalon, and other materials are becoming increasingly popular. Originally they were exceptionally heavy, but improvements have reduced the weight considerably while retaining the ruggedness and durability. Since the synthetic grip stretches to fit, reaming, filing, or tapering of the hole is not necessary and, of course, the grips do not have to be shaped. These synthetics do not chip and can be taken in and out of the rod holders repeatedly without damage.

REEL SEATS

The key to selecting a reel seat is picking the smallest size that will hold the reel on the rod securely. Weight is also a consideration. Heavier reel seats don't make a significant difference on bigger rods, but they add unnecessary weight to lighter casting rods. The reel seat you choose should be corrosion resistant. To avoid corrosion from electrolysis, we prefer quality anodized aluminum seats for all spinning rods, and chrome-plated brass for conventional tackle.

Figure 8. It makes sense to use the best reel seat possible when building your own rod.

A second retaining nut often double locks the reel seat and helps to keep the first nut from backing off while you are fighting a fish. Almost all reel seats have stamped hoods, and these are adequate for most rods. Big-game trolling rods, however, are usually built with machined-hood reel seats because they are stronger and hold the reel more securely.

ROD-WINDING THREADS

Nylon is the most popular type of rod-winding thread currently available. Regular thread has a high sheen and tends to wet out when finish is applied. NCP (No Color Preservative required) or treated thread is a flat-finish, opaque material that does not wet out or become translucent when finish is applied.

Color preserver is a nitrate dope sealer that protects the original thread colors, but does not protect the dyes from fading in sunlight. The same color preserver will help to seal NCP thread and build a smoother finish.

If you plan to use light-color regular thread on a dark blank, run a test. Sometimes, there will be discoloration when the finish is applied—and it is better to find out before you wrap the whole rod.

Underwraps should not be used with light rods, because the extra wrappings add weight and dampen some of the action. When the underwraps are used, the thread size should be chosen carefully. It is very difficult to use a smaller diameter or even the same diameter thread as an overwrap. A larger diameter thread should always be used to overwrap.

Rod-winding threads come in a variety of diameters. The following chart will help to guide your choice.

OO   Very fine. Use for the lightest flyrods.

A   Fine. Popular for underwraps and wrapping guides on light rods.

B   Light. Seldom seen.

C   Medium. About twice as thick as A-thread and popular for wrapping guides.

D   Medium Heavy. Used for guide wraps and overwraps on rods up to medium-size trolling.

E   Heavy. Coarse for light rods, but used on heavier rods.

EE   Extra Heavy. Primary choice for husky trolling rods up to unlimited class.

3. *Building a Rod*

FINDING THE SPLINE

Almost every blank has a "spline" or direction in which the blank tends to bend. Custom rod builders have the advantage of lining up the guides with the spline, and they find it is easy. With the blank angling diagonally in front of you, rest the tip in your right hand so it supports the blank from below. Place the

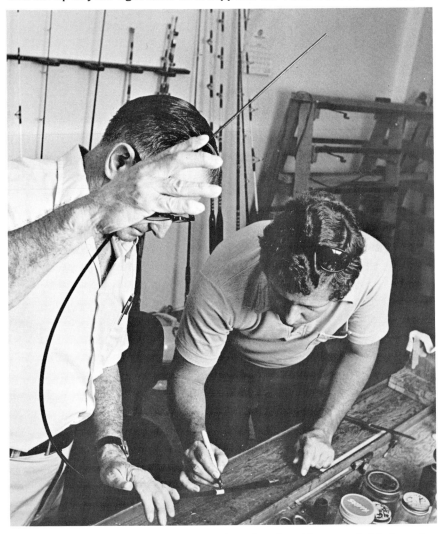

Figure 9. Determine the spline of the blank, and mark it with tape and a felt tip marker so that the guides can be aligned with it.

fingers of the left hand near the center of the blank so they touch it from above. Press down with the left hand and, at the same time, push up with the right hand at the tip without letting the rod fall between the fingers at either point.

Allow the rod to rotate of its own accord. The rod will seem to jump into its spline position. To test, try to turn the blank out of that position with the fingers of either hand. It should resist turning and jump back when released until it is rotated almost 180° (the opposite of the spline).

When the spline has been found, it should be marked with a piece of masking tape. If you sight along the spline, you should detect a slight curve up or down. We prefer to place the guides so that this curve is down when the rod is held in a normal fishing position. The curve should bend toward the direction of the cast, or in the direction of the fish during the fight. A baitcasting rod is cast with the handles of the reel in the up position and some specialists prefer to place the guides on these rods 90° from the spline position so that the rod will be *cast* with the spline toward the direction of the cast. This, of course, is a matter of personal preference.

FERRULING

When storage or packing a rod for travel isn't a problem, many anglers prefer one-piece rods. However, two-piece models are certainly easier to stow and transport. If you want a two-piece rod, the time to do the ferruling is before you attempt any other operation in the rod-building process. You have a choice between using a metal ferrule and internal fiberglass ferruling. Fiberglass ferruling can not be used on every blank, but where it is possible, it is usually the superior method.

Fitting a Metal Ferrule

STEP 1 **(Figure 10).** Slide the female ferrule down the blank until it comes tight. Mark the position on the blank for reference.

STEP 2 **(Figure 11).** Remove the ferrule and hold it against the blank to measure where to make the cut. The blank is usually cut about ⅛ inch below the point where the male section of the ferrule will seat in the female.

STEP 3 **(Figure 12).** The blank should be cut with a fine-toothed hacksaw or a three-cornered file. Remember that metal ferrules come in a number of sizes; it is important to pick the right one.

STEP 4 **(Figure 13).** Install the female side of the ferrule with epoxy glue. To fit the male section, you will have to trim the blank. This should be done a little bit at a time until the male section fits. Use epoxy glue to attach it. Any metal ferrule joint can be strengthened by filling the blank with a short dowel, piece of fiberglass, or even epoxy glue inside the blank under the ferrule sections.

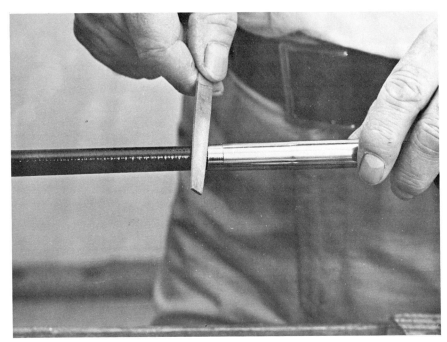

Figure 10.

Figure 11.

18

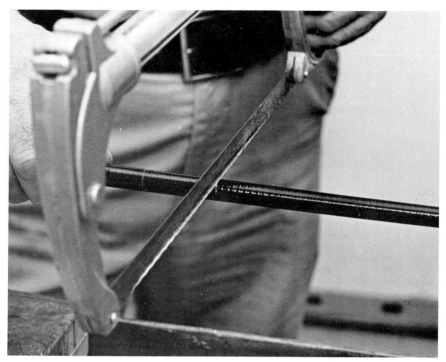

Figure 12.

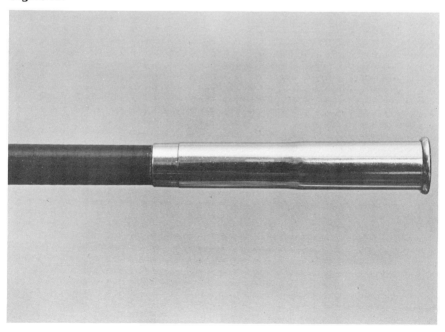

Figure 13.

19

Installing a Fiberglass Ferrule

The fiberglass ferrule offers advantages over metal ferrules because of its light weight, corrosion resistance, flexibility, and the fact that it can be adjusted for wear. Many blanks are now available with factory-installed, fiberglass ferrules. You can install your own internal fiberglass ferrules without difficulty on most rod blanks with excellent results. The same technique is also used for repairing almost any broken fiberglass rod.

To do the job, you must purchase a solid fiberglass blank that matches the approximate taper of the tubular rod you intend to ferrule. The solid blanks are relatively inexpensive and are available from most qualified component dealers. Usually, the solid blank is used for only one ferrule. The left-over pieces can be wound with coarse sandpaper, however, and used as cork reamers.

The blanks most suitable for this type of ferruling have a relatively large inside diameter in relation to their wall thickness. Heavy-wall, narrow-diameter blanks do not retain their strength as well with internal glass ferrules. Here is the basic procedure.

STEP 1 **(Figure 14).** Use a fine-toothed hacksaw to cut the blank where the ferrule is to be installed.

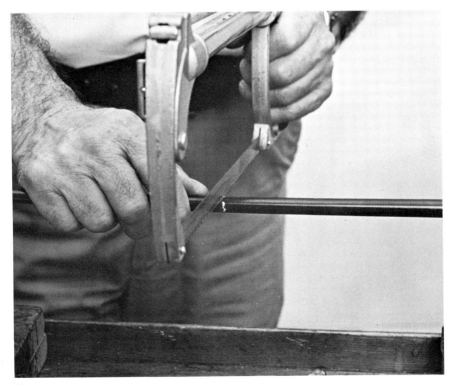

Figure 14.

STEP 2 **(Figure 15).** Using a file, smooth and straighten the ends that were cut.

STEP 3 **(Figure 16).** Hold the butt section of the tubular blank in your left hand with the end that you just filed in front of you. Push the tip (small end) of the solid glass blank into this opening, and slide it all the way in until it comes tight.

STEP 4 **(Figure 17).** With the solid blank seated in the tubular section (Step 3), trim off the remaining butt section of the solid blank. The cut should be made so that a length equal to 4 or 5 times the diameter of the tubular blank at the point where the solid blank enters it, is left extending on the solid blank.

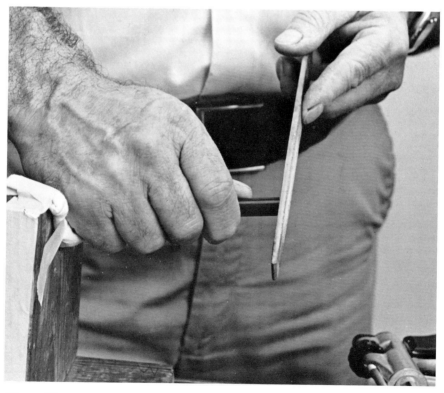

Figure 15.

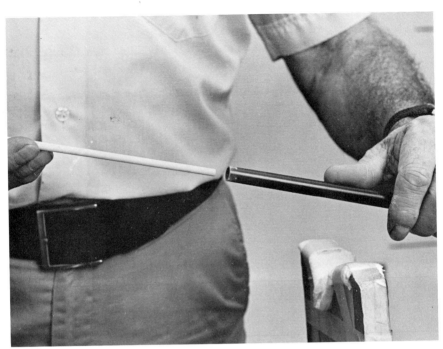

Figure 16.

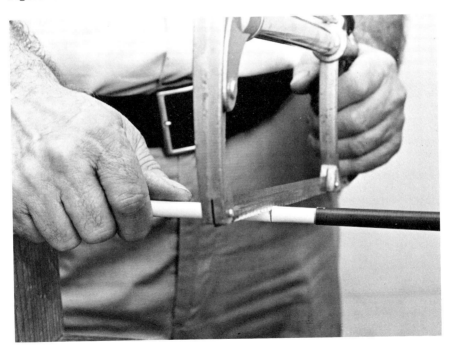

Figure 17.

22

STEP 5 **(Figure 18).** Remove all the solid blank from the tubular section and round the edges on the solid blank at the point where you made the cut in Step 4. By eliminating the sharp edges on the solid blank, you reduce stress concentrations when the finished rod is under pressure.

STEP 6 **(Figure 19).** Spread epoxy glue inside the end of the tubular butt section where the ferrule will sit. Be sure to cover the area thoroughly.

STEP 7 **(Figure 20).** Insert the tip of the solid blank into the butt section of the tubular blank and pull it all the way through until the ferrule is seated. As the solid section starts to fit tightly, twist it gently into place to spread the glue evenly.

Figure 18.

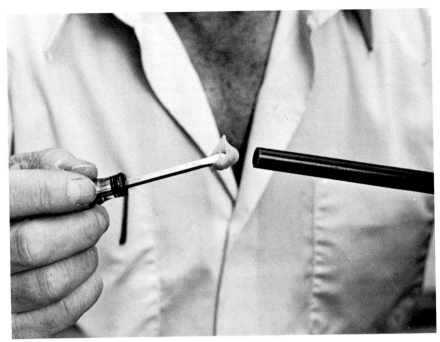

Figure 19.

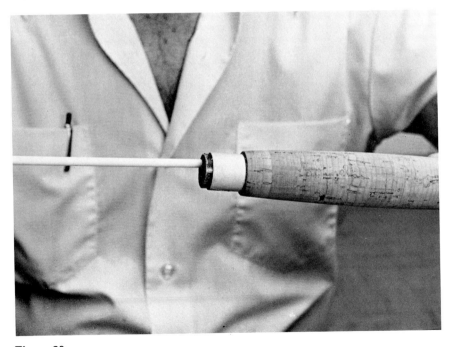

Figure 20.

24

STEP 8 **(Figure 21).**   Trim off the solid ferrule so that about 5 or 6 times its diameter remains extended. After the cut is made, use a file to round the edges just as you did in Step 5.

STEP 9 **(Figure 22).**   Slide the tip section of the tubular blank over the ferrule and check its fit. When the tip is seated tightly, there should be a space between the two sections of about ⅜ inch. On fast taper blanks, the tip will often fit perfectly. On slower action blanks, you may have to trim the tip to make it fit.

STEP 10 **(Figure 23).**   Adjustments to the tip section should be done carefully. Cut off short sections of the tip until the ferrule fits.

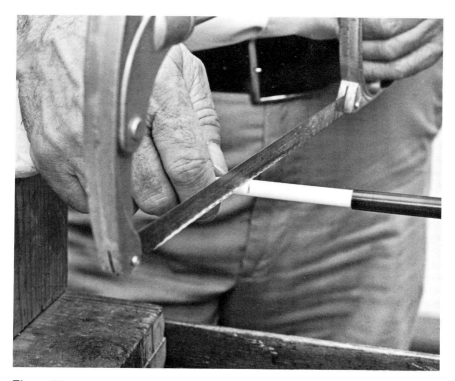

Figure 21.

Figure 22.

Figure 23.

26

STEP 11   **(Figure 24).**   When the tip section fits, you will see about ⅜ inch of the solid ferrule.

STEP 12   **(Figure 25).**   The tubular blank should be wrapped on both sides of the ferrule to strengthen it and prevent splitting. Some rod builders prefer to double-wrap this area.

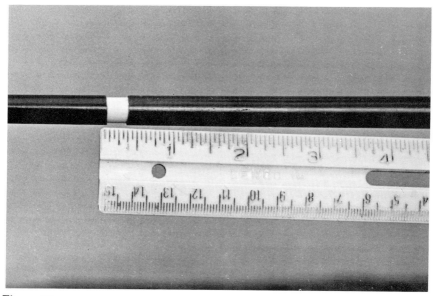

Figure 24.

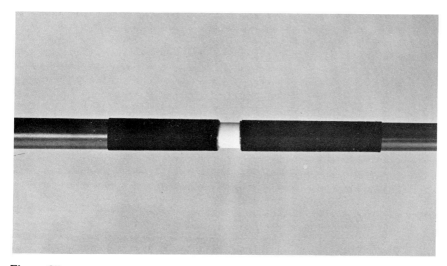

Figure 25.

Mounting Butt Ferrules and Adapters

Both metal butt ferrules for baitcasting rods with conventional detachable casting handles and the plastic adapters for the new speed-type handle systems are available in a wide range of sizes. In fitting these to the butt end of the blank, be sure to leave room for the epoxy glue. If the fit is too loose or if the adapter tilts off center, you can take up the slack by criss-crossing two pieces of thread, fishing line, or string over the end of the blank. A dowel or short length of fiberglass used as a plug under the area where the ferrule or adapter is to be installed will strengthen the connection. Roughen the blank before applying the epoxy, and then twist the ferrule carefully to spread the epoxy evenly.

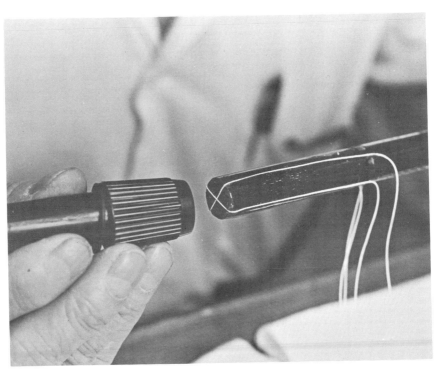

Figure 26. Criss-cross two pieces of thread, fishing line, or string to take up the slack and tighten the fit of a butt ferrule or adapter.

GLUING THE GRIPS IN PLACE

Cork

Whether you use cork rings, sticks or preshaped grips, the center must be reamed out to fit the blank. Actually, to insure proper fit, the grip should stop several inches above the point where it will actually seat when in position. Glue acts as a lubricant and the grip can be pushed into position once the epoxy is applied. Reamers can be made by wrapping coarse sandpaper around pieces of old blank, or you can use a round file. The blank to which rings or grips are to be fitted can be made into a reamer by winding a strip of coarse sandpaper over and over toward the tip section and then taping off both ends. Be sure to rotate the cork as you ream so that the hole will remain round.

Rough up the blank slightly where the cork will be positioned to insure a better bonding surface. Then, spread epoxy well above the point where the grip would fit tightly on a dry blank so that an adequate coating of glue forms inside the grip. This will enable you to push the grip all the way into place. A piece of masking tape wrapped around the end of the blank will keep you from pushing the first grip too far, and leave room for a butt cap.

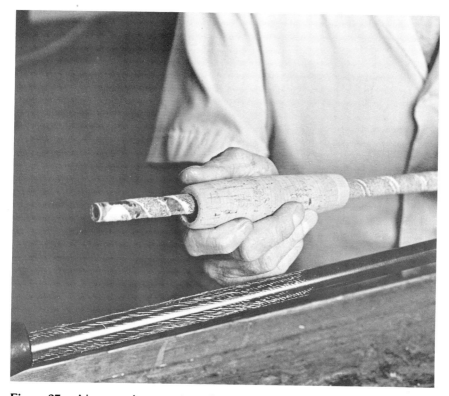

Figure 27. A homemade reamer is used to enlarge the hole in a cork grip. Note that the rod blank has been scored with a file to present a better bonding surface for the glue.

Figure 28. Wrap a ring of masking tape around the butt as a stop for the grip. Coat the blank with epoxy glue several inches above the spot where the grip will ultimately seat and slide the grip into place. A butt cap will later replace the tape.

Preshaped grips and cork sticks are pushed on as a single unit. The ½-inch cork rings must be seated individually. Glue should also be spread on the face of each cork ring so that it seals against each adjoining ring. Compression usually holds these rings together, but some builders use rubber bands or presses to hold the rings until the glue sets.

If you ream the grip too much, epoxy will fill the gap and make a good bond. However, if you go beyond the limits of the epoxy, you can wrap thread, fishing line, or string around the blank to take up the space.

Cork rings and sticks must be shaped when the glue sets. Rough out the basic shape with coarse grit sandpaper such as number 60. Then switch consecutively to number 80, 100, 160, and finally, number 220 to finish the grip.

Cellite and Synthetics

These grips do not require reaming. Instead, they stretch over the blank and grip it tightly. The important aspect of seating these grips is to insure that the blank is coated with epoxy for a considerable distance and the glue is worked into the inside surface of the grip. Then, with a steady motion, the grip can be pushed into place. On fast-taper blanks, some of these synthetic grips have a tendency to creep back up. This can be prevented by winding a ring of masking tape on the blank at the top of the grip.

Removing the excess glue from a blank is not difficult if you follow a basic procedure. Start with a dry rag or a paper towel and make a pass or two over the blank, removing what you can. Go back over the surface again with a moist towel. Finally, dampen a towel with acetone or lacquer thinner and remove the last residue of the glue.

Figure 29. Synthetic grips stretch over the blank. Spread epoxy above the area where the grip first tightens and the remaining length of the blank. Make sure the inside surface gets coated with glue.

Figure 30. The grip is forced down the blank into position with the glue acting as a lubricant. A ring of masking tape at the bottom of the blank serves as a stop.

Figure 31. Excess glue is wiped off the blank with a series of rags or paper towels. The last one is dampened with acetone, lacquer thinner, or other solvent to remove the final residue.

MOUNTING THE REEL SEAT

Fixed Type

Most reel seats have an inside diameter larger that the diameter of the blank on which they are to fit, so it becomes necessary to use a bushing to fill the space. Cork bushings are available for the standard reel seats. These are glued into the reel seat first, allowed to set up, and then reamed to fit the blank. The reaming procedure is identical to that for grips and the hole should be slightly smaller than the blank so that a tight fit will be assured.

If bushings are not available for the reel seat you have selected, you can make your own. Install the butt grip and then wind two or three bands of masking tape around the blank where the reel seat is to be positioned. Leave space between each band of tape. There should be just enough tape so the reel seat fits snugly and barely slides over it.

Use paste-type epoxy glue that is thick enough to stay in place without dripping, and fill the area between the bands of tape. Slide the reel seat into

Figure 32. Wrap masking tape around the threads of the reel seat to avoid getting glue on them. Then, if a commercially made bushing is not available, wind two or three rings of masking tape around the blank where the reel seat will be positioned.

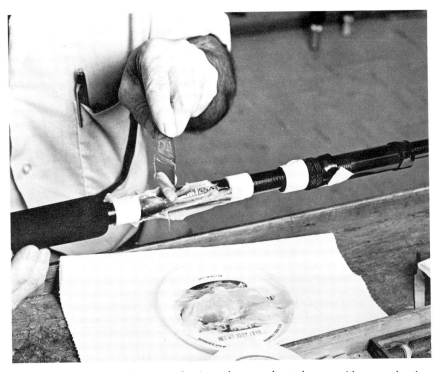

Figure 33. Leave room between the rings of tape, and coat the area with epoxy glue that is thick enough so it won't drip.

position, then put the rod aside until the glue sets. Remember that the fixed hood on the reel seat should be aligned with the spline of the rod.

The permanent bond must be between the blank and the reel seat. Experienced builders roughen up the area inside the reel seat and on the blank for better bonding. If you only apply glue to the tape, the bond will be weak and you will be relying on the tape's "stickum" to hold the reel seat in place.

When you mount a detachable reel seat on a wood or aluminum butt for a trolling rod, roughen the inside of the reel seat, use epoxy glue, and align the fixed hood of the seat with the slots in the butt gimbal. Wood butts, like baseball bats, have the straight grain of the wood in the strongest plane. That is why the straight grain should be lined up with the slot in the stationary hood of the reel seat.

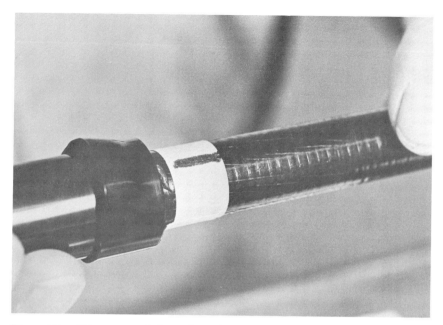

Figure 34. When you push the reel seat into position, be sure to align the fixed hood with the spline mark on the blank.

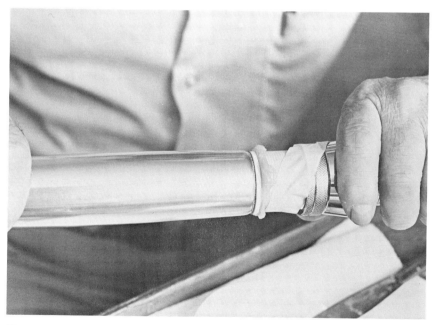

Figure 35. A wood or aluminum trolling rod butt should be glued to the reel seat with epoxy.

Trolling Rods

Tremendous strain is placed on a trolling blank at the point where it fits into the reel seat ferrule on a locking-type reel seat. Some blanks are now manufactured with a built-on fiberglass bushing to fit the appropriate reel seat, and they can be glued into place with epoxy. Some of the best trolling blanks, however, lack the bushings, so that custom builders can trim the butt for a desired length and action.

We have found that fiberglass cloth makes an excellent bushing for these heavier rods. Roughen the blank at the point where the bushing is to be built. Cut a strip of fiberglass cloth so that the width of the cloth matches the approximate length of the reel seat ferrule. Apply epoxy glue to both sides of the fiberglass cloth and wind the glue-impregnated cloth around the blank until it fits the inside diameter of the ferrule. Let the mass harden over night; then sand or file it for a perfect fit. The ferrule can then be glued into place with epoxy. Be sure to align the slot in the fixed hood of the reel seat with the spline mark on the blank.

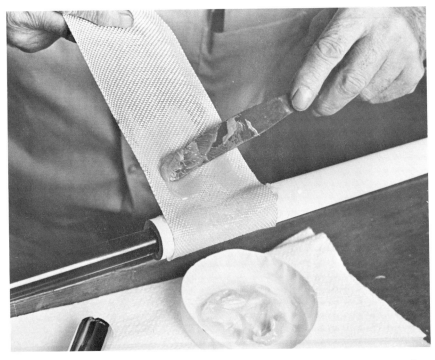

Figure 36. Fiberglass cloth is the best material for fashioning a bushing on a trolling rod. The width of the cloth should match the length of the reel seat. Apply epoxy glue to both sides of the cloth.

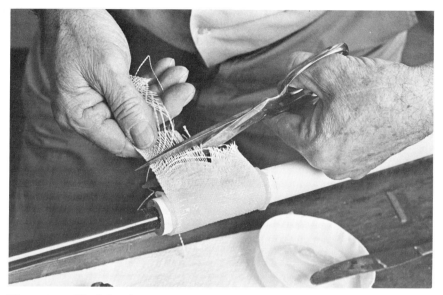

Figure 37. Wind the glue-impregnated cloth around the blank so that it just fits the inside diameter of the reel seat ferrule. Cut off the excess cloth and allow the glue to harden over night.

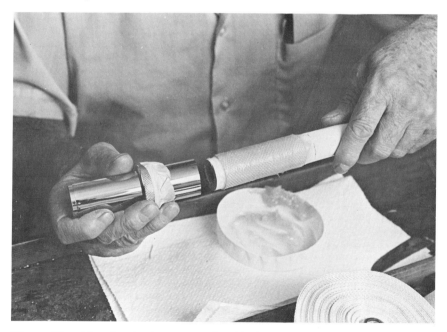

Figure 38. After the glue has set, sand or file the fiberglass cloth bushing until it is smooth and fits inside the ferrule. Apply more epoxy, position the ferrule, and let the glue set.

ATTACHING THE TIPTOP

A good grade of hot melt-tip cement should be used to attach tiptops. Some rod makers prefer epoxy glue; but if the tip must be replaced, the epoxy is extremely difficult to remove. The procedure for installing the tiptop is simple.

STEP 1. Heat the melt-tip cement with a match, lighter, candle, alcohol burner, or propane torch.

Figure 39. Heat some melt-tip cement and apply it to the tip of the blank.

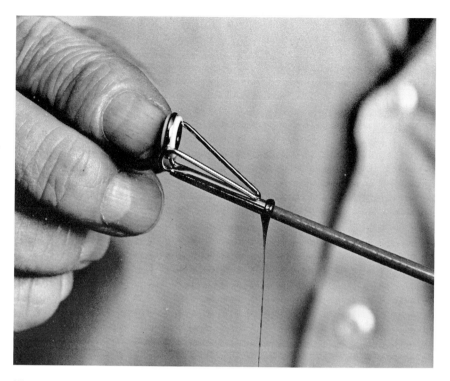

Figure 40. Scrape some melt-tip cement in the tiptop tube, pass the tiptop through the flame, and seat it on the rod. Be sure to align it with the spline and the fixed hood of the real seat.

STEP 2.   Quickly spread the melted cement around the tip of the blank.

STEP 3.   Apply heat to the melt-tip cement that is on the tip of the blank (Step 2) and scrape a little of it into the tube of the tiptop.

STEP 4.   Pass the tiptop through the flame and place it on the rod while it is still warm, aligning it to the spline of the blank and to the fixed hood on the reel seat.

STEP 5.   The blank and the tiptop must not be overheated, or damage could result. Ceramic tiptops, for example, incorporate a plastic shock absorber ring that could shrink or melt if the heat is excessive.

WRAPPING THE GUIDES

Guide Spacing

Properly spaced guides distribute the strain on the blank evenly when it is put into an arc, and they assist the line in its flow from the reel out through the tip during the cast. There is no universal rule for guide spacing that applies to all types of rods. The correct spacing for each will depend on the length of the rod, its taper, and the reel to be used.

The most important measurement is between the face of the reel and the first guide. After that, the distance between each guide will get progressively shorter. Spinning rods and trolling rods should have at least 5 guides and a tiptop. Baitcasting rods require 5 to 7 guides; and flyrods should have a minimum of one guide per foot of length plus the tiptop.

The best approach is to tape the guides in place, put a reel on the rod, rig the line through the guides, and have someone pull on the line so you can check the flow of line through the guides. As a starting point, the distance from the face of the reel to the first guide is about 22 inches on ultra-light spinning, 25 inches on medium spinning, 34 inches on a surf rod about 9 feet long, 17 to 19 inches on baitcasting, and 30 inches on flyrod.

With the rod bent in an arc, the line should move from guide to guide in an even arc. Position the guides so that there are no sharp angles in the line between the guides. You may have to add an extra guide or two. When the flex of the rod is covered, make several casts and look for line slap. If the rod casts well and you can not detect the line hitting the blank, you are ready to wrap the guides in place permanently. Should you find line slap, simply move the first guide back and forth until it is eliminated.

The Basics of Wrapping

Before a guide is placed on the blank, the edges of the feet should be tapered with a flat file and any burrs removed. This insures that the guides will seat flat. Measure the position of each guide and tape it on the blank in line with the spline (which will also align the guides with the fixed hood of the reel seat and the tiptop). Re-read the section on guide spacing, and make certain each guide is properly spaced before beginning to wrap.

STEP 1   **(Figure 41).**   Start an eye-appealing distance in front of the guide foot you want to wrap, and take one turn with the thread around the blank. Hold the tag end in the fingers of one hand and angle it slightly toward the guide while you make the first 4 or 5 wraps crossing the short end of thread each time. This will keep it in place, since knots are not used.

STEP 2   **(Figure 42).**   After making 4 or 5 turns, use a razor blade or sharp scissors to trim the tag end of the thread. Each wrap should be straight and packed closely against the preceding one.

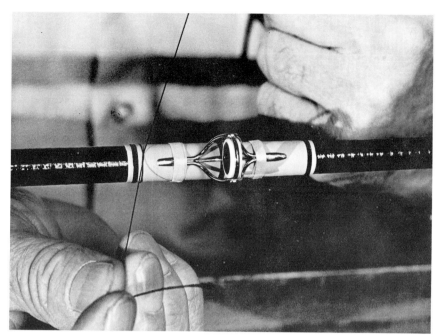

Figure 41.

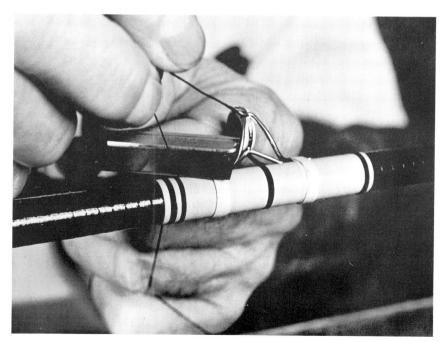

Figure 42.

STEP 3 **(Figure 43).** As the wrap starts to cover the foot of the guide, remove the masking tape on that side and continue to wrap, making sure that each strand lays neatly against the one before it.

STEP 4 **(Figure 44).** About 5 turns before the end of the wrap, insert a loop of thread or light monofilament with the closed end of the loop toward the guide. This is for finishing the wrap without a knot.

STEP 5 **(Figure 45).** After taking about 5 more turns, cut the thread and insert the tag end in the loop. Continue to maintain finger pressure on the wrap so it doesn't loosen while you are finishing it off.

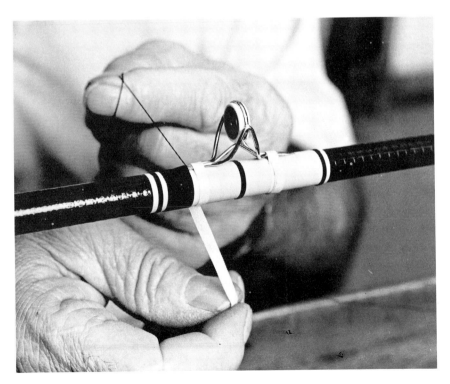

Figure 43.

42

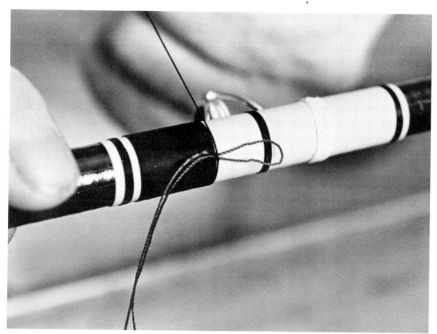

Figure 44.

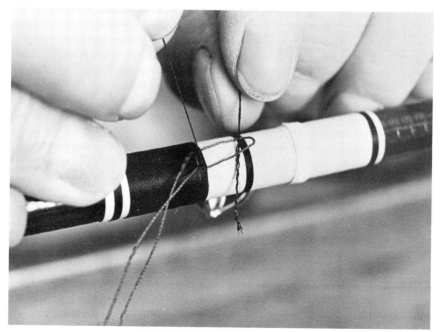

Figure 45.

STEP 6 **(Figure 46).** Using the loop you inserted, pull the tag end of the wrapping thread under the wrap.

STEP 7 **(Figure 47).** Trim the tag end with a sharp razor blade, being careful not to touch the wrap with the blade.

STEP 8 **(Figure 48).** By using the back of the razor blade as a "comb", you can close small gaps in the wrap and even it out.

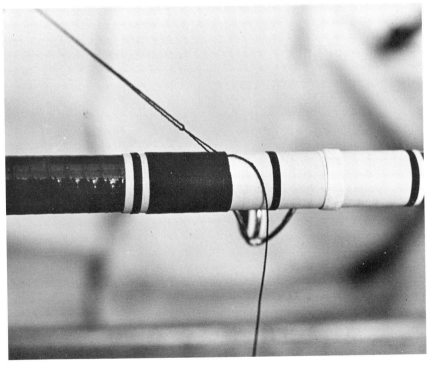

Figure 46.

44

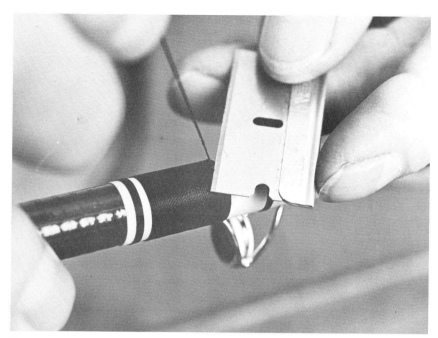

Figure 47.

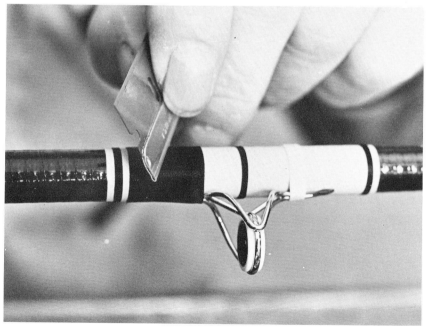

Figure 48.

Tying a Short Trim Wrap

Short trim wraps add a decorative touch to rods and they are done in the same way that the basic wrap is formed. The only difference is that by the time you take a couple of turns to lock the tag end of the thread, you are ready to finish off.

STEP 1 **(Figure 49).**   Start the trim wrap just as you would a regular wrap, but cut off the starting end after 2 or 3 turns. Then, insert the finishing loop.

STEP 2 **(Figure 50).**   Make 3 or 4 more turns, cut the wrapping thread, and insert the end in the loop. Be sure to maintain finger pressure on the wrap so it doesn't unravel.

STEP 3 **(Figure 51).**   Pull the tag end under the wrap and trim with a sharp razor blade.

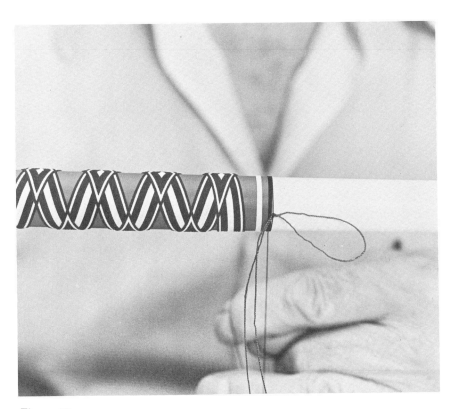

Figure 49.

46

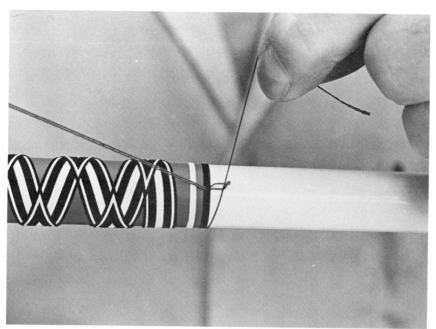

Figure 50.

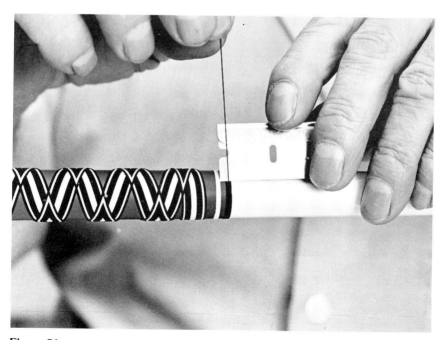

Figure 51.

The Diamond Wrap

The diamond wrap is gaining in popularity as a decorative way to dress up a fishing rod. Once you learn the basic procedure, the intricacy of the patterns you use will only be limited by your imagination and the amount of time you want to spend on it.

STEP 1 **(Figure 52).** Make an underwrap long enough to cover the area under the diamond. If you prefer, the diamond wrap can be done on the blank without the underwrap. Directly on top of the rod and in line with the reel seat and tiptop, mark spaces an equal distance apart the length of the underwrap (we use one inch centers for most rods). On the opposite side of the blank, make another series of dots that are also one inch apart, but these should be started at ½ inch.

STEP 2 **(Figure 53).** If you enjoy doing diamond wraps, you can save time by making a template out of aluminum with holes every inch.

STEP 3 **(Figure 54).** Start with two or three strands of thread and either tape them to the base of the underwrap or wind them around. You don't have to be very neat. because this will be cut off later. Very carefully, spiral the strands of thread around the rod, keeping them flat. You must cross every dot you made in Step 1 on either side of the rod.

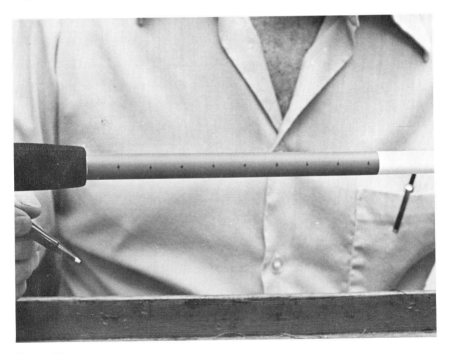

Figure 52.

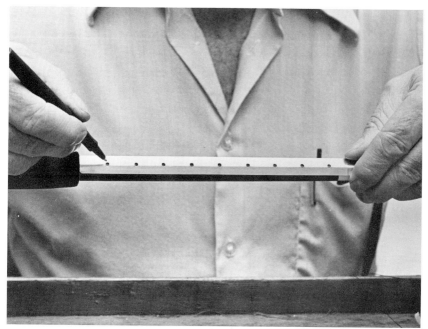

Figure 53.

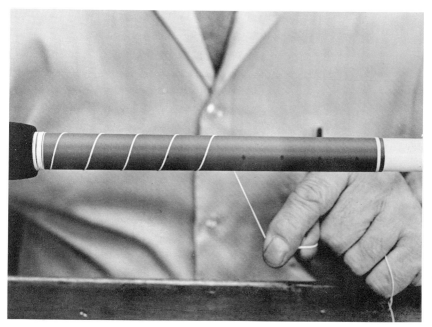

Figure 54.

49

STEP 4 **(Figure 55).** When you reach the end, start back, working toward the starting point.

STEP 5 **(Figure 56).** Either slip the ends of the thread under the tape or hold them with a clothespin after completing the first wrap. Before doing anything else, use you thumb nail or a tool such as a screwdriver to make sure the threads are pushed together and that they cross exactly at the dots.

STEP 6 **(Figure 57).** Two more strands of white thread have been added on either side of the initial pair using the same technique. Two strands of black thread have now been tied in and are being spiraled down the blank.

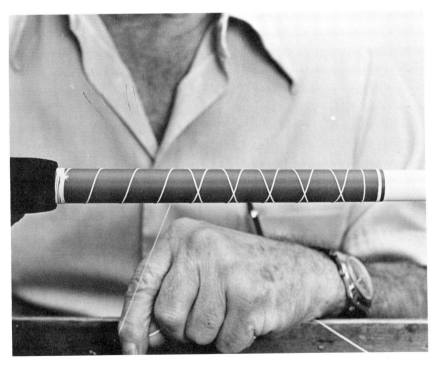

Figure 55.

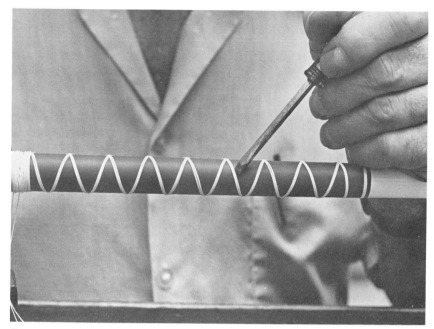

Figure 56.

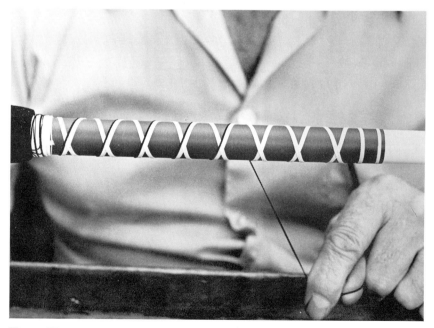

Figure 57.

STEP 7 **(Figure 58).** The black thread is then worked down the other side of the wrap so that the wrap will be even.

STEP 8 **(Figure 59).** As the black band is added to the other side of the white wrappings, the diamond pattern begins to appear.

STEP 9 **(Figure 60).** Four more strands of black have now been added *on each side* of the existing wrap, followed by a band of white on each side and then a final band of black. Either some masking tape or a few wraps from the final thread will hold the jumble of threads together near the base. Carefully trim the ends with a razor blade or scissors.

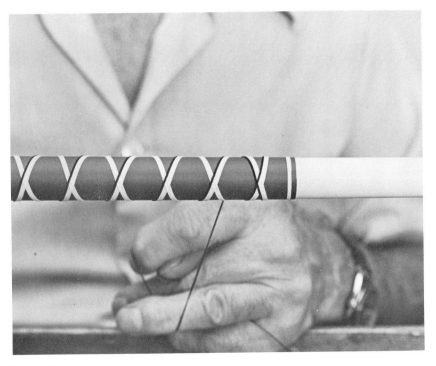

Figure 58.

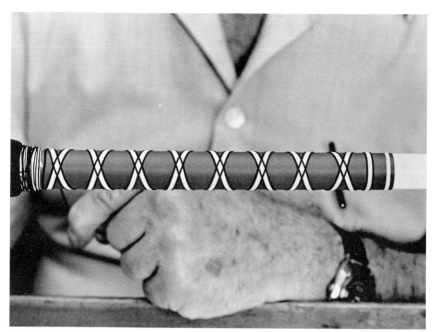

Figure 59.

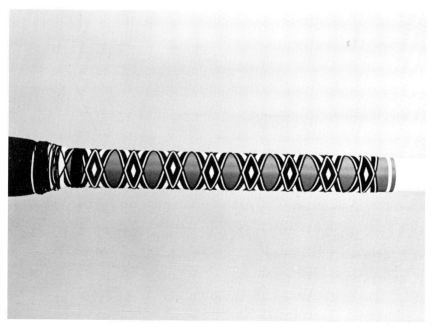

Figure 60.

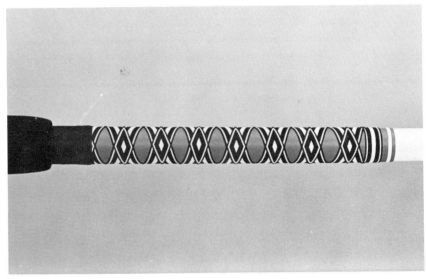

Figure 61.

STEP 10 **(Figure 61).** After trimming away the excess thread at the base of the diamond wrap, finish filling in the butt wrap to cover the ends. It may require a double winding to achieve a neat appearance. The rod is now ready to be finished.

The Double Chevron Wrap

The double chevron is a complicated, but very impressive looking wrap that is not really hard to do, but it does require patience and care to keep all of the criss-crosses in perfect alignment. Note that the wrap is started in 4 places around the rod, 90° apart. We recommend that you master the diamond wrap first, before attempting the double chevron.

STEP 1 **(Figure 62).** Starting at the top of the rod and in line with the guides, mark a row of evenly spaced reference dots. An underwrap can be used, or you can put the double chevron directly on the blank. For most rods, we recommend that these dots be ¾ inch apart. Now rotate the rod 90° and mark another set of dots in the same relative positions as the first dots. Repeat this procedure two more times until you have four sets of evenly spaced dots. They do not have to be staggered as you did in the diamond wrap. Tie in two or three strands of thread and spiral them along the blank crossing *every other dot* in any single row of dots.

STEP 2 **(Figure 63).** Then work back toward the butt crossing the same dots you crossed in the first pass. At the forward end of the underwrap, it's a good idea to wrap some tape on the blank to prevent the threads from marring the finish.

54

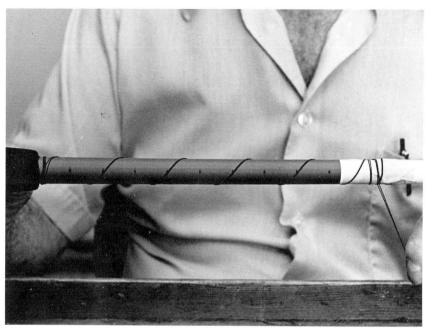

Figure 62.

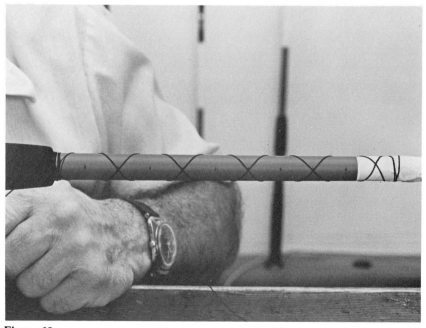

Figure 63.

STEP 3 **(Figure 64).** Rotate the rod 90° and start another band of black, following the same procedure you did in Step 2.

STEP 4 **(Figure 65).** Turn the rod 90° more and repeat Step 2. Finally, rotate the rod another 90°, and repeat Step 2. You have now covered all of the dots you marked in Step 1.

STEP 5 **(Figure 66).** The first color is widened by adding another band alongside the original wraps. Remember you have to rotate the rod 4 times and use 4 separate sets of threads.

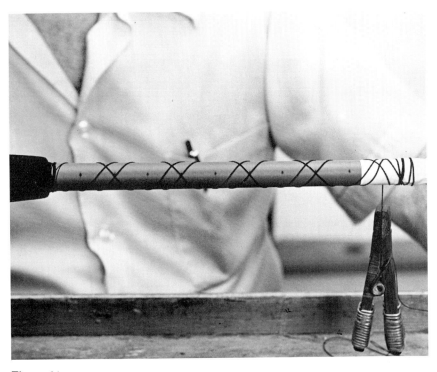

Figure 64.

Figure 65.

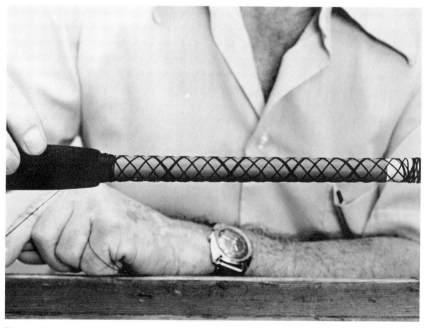

Figure 66.

STEP 6 **(Figure 67)**. At this point, pause and examine the wraps. Straighten and align any that are off center and close any gaps between the wraps.

STEP 7 **(Figure 68)**. A second color is now introduced, following the basic procedure outlined in Step 2. Notice that the new band is added only to one side of the original band rather than to both sides as in the diamond wrap.

STEP 8 **(Figure 69)**. The third color is added and spiraled as outlined in Step 7. In this case, only a single white band was used instead of the double bands of the first two colors. When you have wrapped the final color up and back, you are ready to finish off.

Figure 67.

58

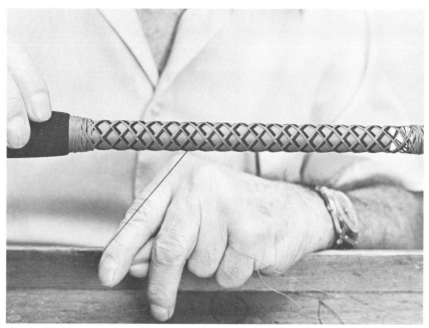

Figure 68.

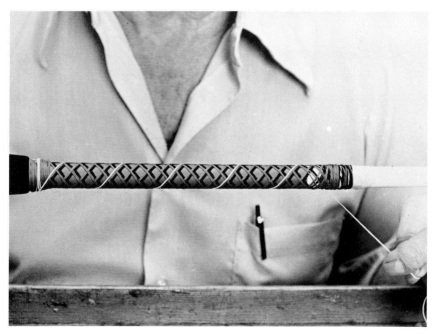

Figure 69.

STEP 9 **(Figure 70).** Use tape or a few turns of the final color to hold the ends of the threads in place while you trim them neatly with scissors or a razor blade.

STEP 10 **(Figure 71).** A short wrap at each end of the chevron gives the decorative trim a finished appearance.

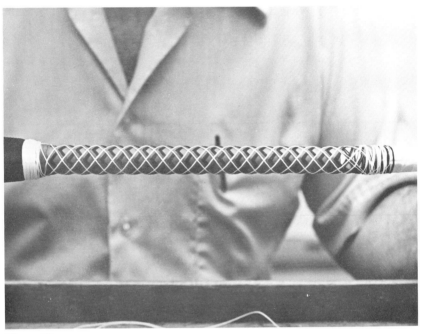

Figure 70.

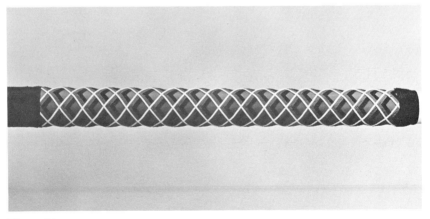

Figure 71.

FINISHING THE ROD

Choosing the Finish

A good finish should be flexible enough to give with the rod as it bends and yet hard enough to withstand abrasion. The finish should fill the hills and valleys created by the thread winds so that the surface feels smooth when the thumb nail is run down the wrap. If the finish is too thin, the threads will be exposed to fraying, abrasion, and ultimately, unraveling. Most rod blanks have their own finish and do not require any additional treatment except for the wrappings on the guides and any decorative wraps you may add.

With the exception of NCP or specially treated types of threads, new wrappings should be coated with color preserver first to seal the thread and help it retain its original color. If you do use color preserver, apply several coats, allowing each to dry before applying the next. Some rod builders omit the preserver, with the result that the regular thread becomes darker and slightly translucent. The varnish, polymer, or epoxy finish gives the windings an exceptionally strong bond.

NCP thread greatly simplifies the operation, because it is opaque and can be used successfully in light colors over dark blanks without showing the blank through the thread. Final finish can be applied directly over the wrap.

Depending on the diameter of the thread (thin threads cover more easily), it may require 4 to 10 coats of a good varnish to obtain a smooth finish. Most varnishes require over night drying between coats; and, towards the last few coats, some light sanding helps.

Thick epoxy and polymer finishes can be applied in one or two coats. Label directions refer to the entire container and, if you use smaller quantities, you may have to add a little more or less hardener.

Applying the Finish

One of the popular polymer finishes that we prefer requires a 50/50 mixture. Since the material sets up so quickly, we prefer to mix very small batches. Using a baby food jar as a mixing vessel, a plastic picnic spoon is filled level with hardener (but not overflowing). The hardener is then emptied into the jar and the spoon discarded. Resin material is poured into another spoon, but this time the spoon is allowed to just barely overflow. Both parts are mixed thoroughly and the material is ready to use.

Each wrap should be covered completely with finish. Brush the mixture on the wraps going around and around. Then use longitudinal strokes to insure full coverage. Excess finish can be removed by rotating the rod against a rag or a finger.

Figure 72. Small quantities of epoxy or polymer finishes can be mixed in baby food jars using plastic spoons. You may have to add more or less hardener than recommended when working with smaller quantities.

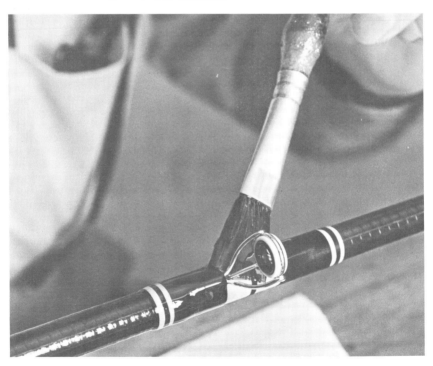

Figure 73. Brush around and around when applying the finish, making sure each part of the wrap is covered including the area under the guide.

Figure 74. After the initial brushing, use longitudinal strokes to insure complete coverage.

Figure 75. Excess finish can be removed easily by rotating the blank against your finger or a rag.

Drying Techniques

If the rod is left in one position, the finish will flow and set up with a blister-type sag on the down-side. To avoid this, the rod must be turned the instant the material begins to sag. Most rod builders eventually rig up an old barbecue motor that will turn slowly and keep the rod rotating while the finish dries evenly. No matter how the rod is rotated, it must be kept level to prevent the finish from flowing to one end of the wraps or the other.

Certain epoxy finishes and even some polymers sometimes react with some color preservers and cause yellowing the first time the wraps are exposed to sunlight. If this problem occurs, substitute three or four coats of Elmer's Glue thinned with water to a brushing consistency for the color preserver, or seal off the color preserver with one coat of varnish. NCP thread without a color preserver will avoid this problem.

4. Rod-building Tips

FLYRODS

Too many guides or guides that are too heavy can easily turn a delicate flyrod into a sluggish casting tool. Tape the guides on the rod before wrapping and try some practice casts or at least move the rod back and forth. Check the rod for a soft and "noodley" action. When you stop moving the rod, the tip should cease oscillating and come to rest with the minimum of vibration.

Fancy wraps and double wraps *at the butt* have little affect on a flyrod, but double wraps farther up the blank may have the same effect as heavier guides. Wraps should be with fine thread and as short as possible. The optimum number of guides varies, but a rule of thumb is that there should be at least one guide per foot of flyrod. Thus, a 7-foot rod would have a minimum of 7 guides.

Reel seats on most light flyrods are mounted with the fixed hood at the butt of the rod so that nothing extends behind the reel to interfere with the line while casting. Extension butts are sometimes added on heavier rods and, when they are used, the reel seat is sometimes turned around. We recommend a 2-inch extension butt if one is to be used.

The sequence for assembling a flyrod follows.

STEP 1.   Find the spline of the blank, and mark it on a piece of tape above the handle area.

STEP 2.   Mount the reel seat on the blank. If a fixed extension butt is to be used, install it before mounting the reel seat.

STEP 3.   Put the grip in place. We recommend cork because it transmits the feel of the cast better than softer materials do.

STEP 4.   Space the guides and tape them on. The stripper guide should be a comfortable reach with the left hand when the rod is in fishing position.

STEP 5.   Mount the tiptop with hot-melt glue.

STEP 6.   After testing the position of the guides, wrap them using the thinnest thread with which you can work. Keep the wraps as short as possible.

STEP 7.   Apply the finish, being careful not to build it up too heavily.

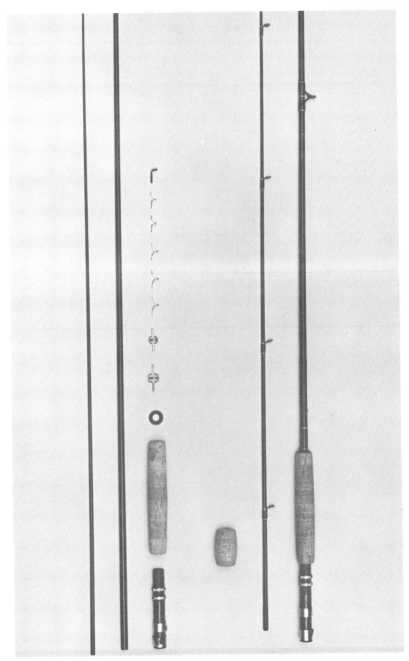

Figure 76. The completed flyrod was made using speed stripper guide and 1 foot speed guides. Also pictured are parts to build a similar rod with 2 stripping guides and the more traditional snake guides.

ULTRA-LIGHT SPINNING RODS

The very lightest spinning rods are constructed with an all-cork handle and sliding rings or a sliding reel seat. The handle is generally flared or capped at both ends to prevent the rings from slipping off. Prefinished grips of this type come in two equal parts. The rear portion is fitted to the blank, rings put on, and the front section seated. Some ultra-light enthusiasts don't even bother with rings. They simply tape their reels to the grip.

For best casting with an ultra-light rod, the gathering guide (first guide) should be placed 24 inches from the front of the reel, give or take an inch or two depending on the brand of the reel. We recommend 4 guides for rods less than 5½ feet long, 5 guides for rods up to 7 feet, and 6 guides for longer rods. The gathering guide or butt guide is always installed first; then the other guides are placed in a descending progression so that the rod bends evenly with no undue strain on the line.

SPINNING RODS

These are built basically the same way as the ultra-light rods, but they usually have a rear grip, fixed reel seat, and foregrip. Spacing for the butt guide is 26 inches from the face of the reel, plus or minus an inch or two depending on reel size. For longer spinning rods, the distance might range to 32 inches and even longer with surf rods. Tape the guides on and move them back are forth until you find the proper spacing.

Here is the assembly sequence:

STEP 1.   Find the spline of the blank and mark it with tape above the reel seat area.

STEP 2.   Install the rear grip and the butt cap.

STEP 3.   Position the reel seat and line up the fixed hood with the spline. We prefer to have the fixed hood forward on the rod, but you could reverse it if it is more comfortable.

STEP 4.   Wrap the guides and install the tiptop.

STEP 5.   Apply the finish to the wraps.

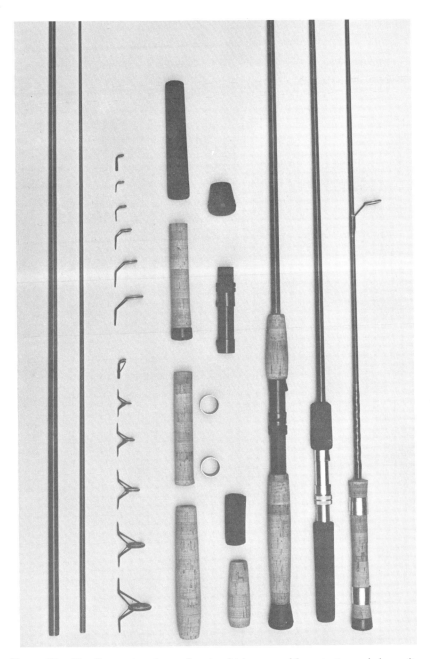

Figure 77. Handle construction and parts which are used for spinning rods from ultra light to medium heavy. Sliding rings are used on some light and ultra light rods to save weight. Fixed reel seats are used on most rods to hold the reel securely. The light colored grips are cork while the dark grips are the new synthetic Cellite material.

POPPING RODS

A popping rod is a baitcasting stick that is built with the blank running straight through like a spinning rod. The handle is not offset as it is on a standard baitcasting rod and the reel seat often has a trigger. Since the foot on most casting reels is chromed brass, the rods should have a chromed brass reel seat. The fixed hood of the reel seat is positioned toward the butt of the rod when there is a trigger. The first guide is usually about 15 inches from the top of the seat, with the spacing of the other guides evenly descending. A 6 foot rod should have 6 guides and 7 guides should be used on rods of 7 feet. The assembly procedure is identical to that for the spinning rod.

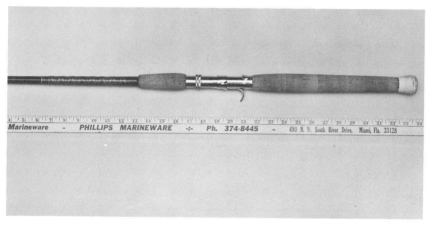

Figure 78.   Handle construction of a popping rod showing "trigger" reel seat.

SOLID GLASS BOAT AND TROLLING RODS

Assembly of these rods is like that of spinning and popping rods except that solid glass blanks are used, for which there are straight-bored wood butt sections that can be epoxy-glued from front or rear with a tenon for reel seat mounting. If the tenon is cut off, smaller reel seats can be used and mounted just as they would be on a spinning rod.

Boat rods usually require a guide for at least every foot of length beyond the reel seat, spaced like those of a popping rod. Trolling rods seldom require more than 5 roller guides or 6 to 7 conventional guides if roller guides are not used. The first should be place at 22 to 24 inches from the top of the reel seat.

Cellite grips are an excellent choice for this type of rod, because they do not chip or get chewed up in rod holders. If a gimbal is used, it is put on the blank after finding the spline and the notches must be lined up with the spline.

Solid glass rods can not be crushed like tubular rods and the solid rods are more resistant to breakage from hitting a boat or bridge rail. Thus they are very popular with party boat operators and charter boatmen because of their exceptional durability.

Most solid glass blanks are shipped unfinished. These blanks can be dressed up considerably by brushing or spraying on two coats of paint of the same color as the blank. Epoxy paint is the best choice for this work. Be sure that the paint is thoroughly dry before assembling the rod.

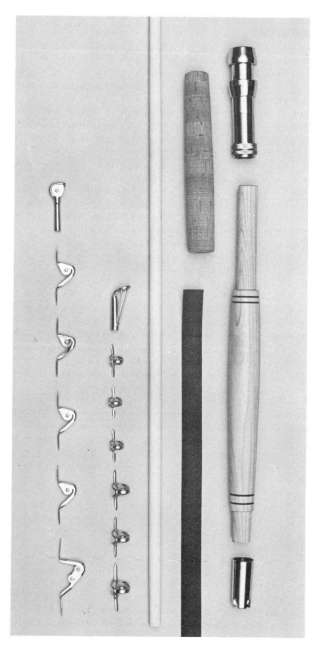

Figure 79. Parts for a solid glass "1 piece" construction boat rod. The butt is bored to fit the blank so that the blank slides all the way through and is set into place with epoxy. A strip of naugahyde, leather, felt, or cork tape is sometimes wound over the foregrip for appearance or durability.

SURF RODS

The actual construction of a surf rod is the same as any other spinning or conventional rod. However, some anglers prefer cork tape or cord in place of the standard grips and reel seat, using tape to attach the reel. To determine the proper length of the grips, extend your arm and place the butt of the blank in your armpit. The center of the reel seat should be at the point where the hand touches the blank.

Many rod builders feel that three shorter grips look better than an arm-long length of cork or synthetic material. Three grips of 5 to 6 inches in length are used, with one placed at the butt of the rod, the second behind the reel seat, and the third in front of the reel seat. The space between the two lower grips can be left bare or finished off with decorative wrapping. If you decide to use cork tape, be sure to wrap over both ends with heavy thread or cord to prevent unraveling.

On spinning and conventional surf sticks, 4 to 6 guides are usually sufficient because too many guides add line friction to these casting tools. The first guide on a spinning surf rod is usually 32 to 36 inches above the reel seat. On a conventional surf rod, 24 to 28 inches is an effective distance for the first guide.

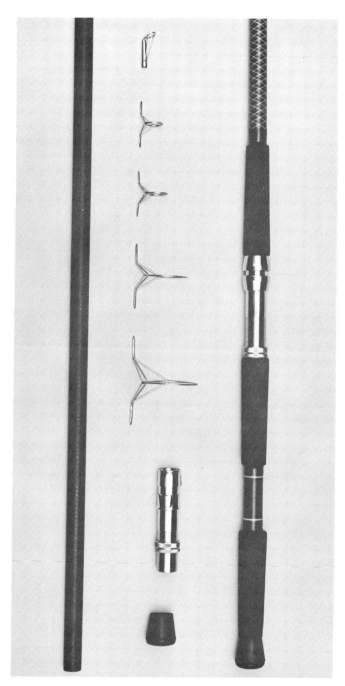

Figure 80. A set of 3 6-inch Cellite grips are used on this heavy surf spinning rod.

TROLLING RODS WITH DETACHABLE BUTTS

Finding the spline of a trolling rod is particularly important so that it won't twist while fighting a big fish. Some rod builders prefer to attach the tiptop temporarily after the spline has been located to help in aligning the reel seat. Once the blank is readied to receive the reel seat ferrule, the ferrule should be locked in the seat before gluing in place, so that the spline of the rod can be aligned with the fixed hood on the reel seat.

If you used the tiptop as a guide for aligning the ferrule, you will have to remove it before sliding the foregrip into place. The reel seat should be separated from the ferrule before installing the foregrip and wrapping the guides.

After the guides have been wrapped, the butt can be glued into the reel seat. This is particularly helpful with an aluminum butt that has the gimbal notches machined in. Epoxy glue is the first choice for securing either wood or aluminum butts to the reel seat and for attaching a gimbal to a wooden butt.

Because of the strain on the glued joint, many builders like to pin reel seats and gimbals to wood butts. This is done by drilling a hole through the gimbal or reel seat and the butt. A Monel boat nail is driven through and then cut off. It is filed flush on both sides.

Aluminum butts should not be pinned to brass reel seats, because this creates an electrical bridge that will eventually destroy both the seat and the butt through electrolysis. If wood butts are used, select a good quality (hickory is best) and line up the straight grain of the wood with the guides for maximum strength. Boat and trolling rods require an extra-heavy finish to protect the wrappings from hard use aboard a boat.

Roller guides reduce friction and line wear on a trolling rod, providing they turn freely. After the rod is finished, check to make sure that epoxy or polymer is not binding any of the roller guides, and keep them clean and lubricated throughout the life of the rod.

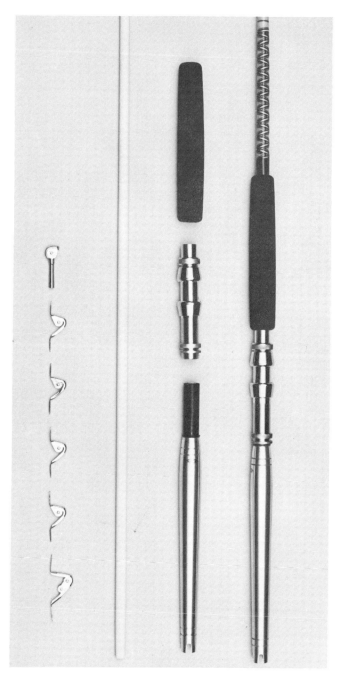

Figure 81. Parts for a first class "regulation" trolling rod are shown with aluminum butt, roller guides and roller tiptop. This is one of the simplest types of rod to build.

5. A Final Word

This manual has been designed to get you started in rod building. It is not intended to be the final word on the subject, but simply a guide to help you establish your own techniques and own way of doing things. By now, you have joined a rapidly growing group of anglers who take pride in custom building their own rods, and you know the feeling of satisfaction that comes from putting the finished product to the test.

New materials and new methods will be developed in the years to come, but once you understand the basics, keeping abreast of changes is easy. Welcome to the ranks of the custom rod builder.   —J.B.E.

6. Index

J. Lee Cuddy ASSOCIATES INC.

offers a complete selection of component parts for rods.

MAIL THIS PAGE

Along with $1.00 to receive our new catalog and price list.

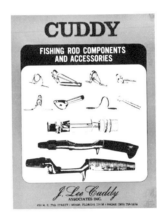

Send the Cuddy catalog to:

Name _____

Street or Box Number _____

City _____State_____Zip Code_____

Mail this page along with $1.00 to: *J. Lee Cuddy*
ASSOCIATES INC.

450 N.E. 79th St.
Miami, Florida   33138